The Great Economic Mysteries Book:

A Guide to Teaching Economic Reasoning Grades 4-8

National Council
on Economic Education

THE **Economics**America AND **Economics**International PROGRAMS

Project Director

Mark C. Schug
University of Wisconsin-Milwaukee
Center for Economic Education

Writers

Mark C. Schug
University of Wisconsin-Milwaukee
Center for Economic Education

Richard D. Western
University of Wisconsin-Milwaukee
Department of Curriculum and Instruction

Production

Diana Borders
Desktop Publishing & Design

Reviewers

Bonnie T. Meszaros
University of Delaware
Center for Economic Education and Entrepreneurship

John S. Morton
Arizona Council on Economic Education

Field Test Teachers

Mary Brenzel-Chavez
Milwaukee Education Center
Milwaukee, Wisconsin

Jenny Keats
Roosevelt School
Wauwatosa, Wisconsin

Amy M. Sutliff
Desert Mountain High School
Scottsdale, Arizona

ISBN 1-56183-125-5

CONTENTS

Economic reasoning proceeds from basic assumptions about human behavior — made credible by historical evidence — to describe and explain human economic activity. *The Great Economic Mysteries Book: A Guide to Teaching Economic Reasoning Grades 4-8,* is part of a new two-volume set from the National Council on Economic Education (NCEE) which aims to introduce students to the "economic way of thinking" through intriguing mysteries from everyday life.

The Great Economic Mysteries Book. A Guide to Teaching Economic Reasoning, Grades 4-8, contains activities that are interactive, reflecting the belief that students learn best through active, highly personalized experiences with economics. Students solve each mystery by responding to hints provided by simple true/false questions and by reference to a logical system of reasoning that applies basic principles of economics. Applications of economic understanding to real-world situations dominate the lessons.

The Great Economic Mysteries Book: A Guide to Teaching Economic Reasoning Grades 4-8, provides teachers with an overview of economic thinking; a model lesson plan for grades 4-8; a guide that states the solution to each mystery; and 17 delightful and often humorous mysteries. Sample mystery titles include "Why Stay Up When It Wipes You Out the Next Day", "The Homework Mystery", and "Why is the Lunchroom Always Dirty". The mysteries, lessons, and activities are correlated to the *Voluntary National Comment Standards in Economics,* which were developed and published by NCEE in 1997.

NCEE is grateful to the authors, Mark C. Schug, Professor of Curriculum and Instruction, and Director of the Center for Economic Education, and Richard D. Western, Associate Professor of Curriculum and Instruction, both at the University of Wisconsin-Milwaukee. NCEE also thanks the Wisconsin Council on Economic Education for its assistance in administering the project.

Since 1949, the National Council on Economic Education, a nonprofit, nonpartisan organization, has been dedicated to increasing the economic literacy of *all* students. This publication builds on five decades of success in delivering economic education in the nation's schools.

Robert F. Duvall, Ph.D.
President and CEO
National Council on Economic Education

This is a book about economic reasoning as it might be taught and practiced in upper-elementary and middle school classrooms. It explains and illustrates a particular approach to reasoning. It shows how students can use this approach to think about problems and to imagine solutions for them. It presents an array of problems, or mysteries, to be used by students in practicing reasoning skills, and it invites teachers and students to supply new mysteries of their own, for extended practice. The field testing we have done to date suggests that many young people especially enjoy moving on to this step—from the given mysteries to ones they've come up with themselves.

Some of the mysteries we present will be familiar to students, reflecting aspects of their experience. Others will challenge students to stretch and think about new things. To help in these efforts, we've built some background information into the problems, in the form of clues or true-false questions. Teachers will decide according to their own circumstances, of course, whether this background information needs to be amplified in particular cases. But we hope nobody will use the mysteries merely as prompts for engaging young people in routine tasks of gathering information. The key to economic reasoning is reasoning, not looking things up.

Reasoning never goes unaccompanied, however. On any occasion that calls for reasoning—in thinking about whether the next pitch will be a curve or a fastball, whether to take the dog for a walk now or after the evening news—all of us try to use what we already know, reasoning from it as a starting point. Experts working in academic and professional fields do the same thing, making deliberate use of their special knowledge. That is why it is never enough to teach students to use generic problem-solving steps. There is no generic procedure for describing problems or brainstorming solutions to them. The describing and brainstorming done in any case will depend, for good or ill, on the outlook and knowledge the problem-solver brings to the task.

Fortunately, in trying to improve our own reasoning skills and in helping children to improve theirs, it isn't necessary to start from scratch. Teachers and children can benefit from the achieved insights of others. If that were not so, nobody could move beyond what Howard Gardner calls the condition of the unschooled mind.

Not surprisingly, the insights featured in *The Great Economics Mysteries Book* are ones formulated originally by economists. We have summarized them in a brief list of principles called the *Handy Dandy Guide*, or sometimes just the *HDG*. These principles represent, in shorthand fashion, the outlook and special knowledge that economists bring to bear on reasoning tasks. In using the *HDG* to describe mysteries and explain them, students begin learning what some people have called the economic way of thinking. It is a way of thinking that can open young people's eyes to new ways of understanding their own world and the public world we expect them, one day, to govern. And, many students say, it is about as much fun as you can have in school.

CHAPTER 1

Economic Reasoning for Kids: An Overview

Is Economics Your Worst Nightmare?

Is the thought of teaching economics your worst nightmare? If it is, you are not alone. Many smart, capable teachers feel the same way. Even those who enjoy teaching government, history, and geography may regard economics as a subject scarier than witches and goblins on Halloween. What might explain this attitude? Is economics inherently remote, dense, and dry?

Not at all. Not necessarily, at least. At key moments in history, economists often have addressed themselves to the analysis of problems that were anything but remote or dry. Adam Smith, the founder of economics, had much to say in 1776 about the most pressing issues of his day—explaining, for example, how trade and the division of labor can increase a nation's prosperity, and arguing that, for Great Britain, the costs of maintaining the American colonies would prove to outweigh the benefits. John Maynard Keynes, seeking to understand and ameliorate the widespread unemployment Great Britain experienced after World War I, argued that deficit spending by governments during periods of recession can foster economic growth and help to bring a nation back to full employment. In subsequent years his theory has been a powerful influence among policy makers in Europe and the United States. During the Great Depression, economists in the United States played an important role in Washington, advising presidents and legislators on policy issues related to labor, agriculture, taxation, corporate monopolies, and welfare. Still more recently, economists have been in the thick of things in the former Soviet Union, advising people there about on-going efforts to modernize the former Soviet-style economies.

But despite this history of engagement with real-world affairs, economics does strike many students today as remote and difficult. In one sense, this is not surprising. After all, economics has been around for a while. It is a mature academic discipline now, one about which economists can speak in detail and at great length—think of all those weighty Econ 101 textbooks! Not only that: as the discipline has matured, economists have sought to be ever more precise in their work, and their search for precision has led them increasingly to the use of rigorous, abstract language, including the language of mathematical operations and models. Macroeconomics, the branch of economics that focuses on whole economic systems, and the branch about which economists tend most to disagree, has become particularly abstract. As a result, even students in Econ 101 now are apt to encounter technical analyses, expressed in compressed, quantitative terms, where they may have expected to find advice about personal finance or general discussions about wealth and poverty.

Where does this leave you? Fortunately, K-12 teachers trying to find their bearings in economics need not choose between the work of Adam Smith and John Maynard Keynes, on the one hand, and the work of technical specialists, on the other. Between the history of economics and its presence in cutting-edge research today, educators can find an impressive set of concepts and principles representing the best insights of the discipline and suitable at the same time for use in curricular planning and day-to-day classroom teaching.

What might these fundamental concepts and principles be? Here are some examples taken from the *Voluntary National Content Standards in Economics* (1997), published by the National Council on Economic Education.

- Productive resources are limited. Therefore, people cannot have all the goods and services they want; as a result, they must choose some things and give up others.

- Effective decision making requires comparing the additional costs of alternatives with the additional benefits. Most choices involve doing a little more or a little less of something; few choices are all-or-nothing decisions.
- Different methods can be used to allocate goods and services. People acting individually or collectively through government must choose which methods to use to allocate different kinds of goods and services.
- People respond predictably to positive and negative incentives.
- Voluntary exchange occurs only when all participating parties expect to gain. This is true for trade among individuals or organizations within a nation, and among individuals or organizations in different nations.

Look back at these five statements and notice what it is that they address: the limits people encounter in striving to satisfy their desires, their need for making choices, the consequences that follow from choosing, the dynamics underlying their transactions with others. Nothing remote or dry in this list of basic human concerns. In the chapters that follow, we'll seek to elaborate that point: economics takes as its subject matter the choices and relationships that matter most to people in their everyday lives.

Right now, however, we want to dwell for a moment on something else you may have noticed about the five statements. The statements have an *edge* to them. Each one *asserts* something: Productive resources *are* limited, voluntary trade occurs *only* when . . ., and so on. The assertions might seem to ring true or false, but they strike few people as bland or inconsequential. They have a probative quality. They cause us to sit up and take notice—to begin thinking about what would follow, in a given case, if one of the statements applied to it.

This assertive, probative quality of our five examples reveals something important about the economic way of thinking. In approaching problems and thinking them through, economists do not start from scratch. They work instead from definite points of departure and they make use of well-established tools in their analyses. They are not only willing but eager, in other words, to work from their disciplinary vantage point.

Doesn't their work violate, then, the norms of objectivity that we associate with honest inquiry and objectivity? Only if you assume that honesty and objectivity depend upon a certain sort of *starting point*—starting with a blank slate or an open mind, setting aside all your assumptions, and so forth. Like most other people who work within academic disciplines, economists do not believe that objectivity in this sense is ever achievable, and they do not seek it. Their norm of objectivity is different. It has to do with facing up to evidence. It is one thing to use established assumptions to get started reasoning out a problem; it is another to check your reasoning against some sort of evidence and to admit that you were wrong if the evidence says you were.

Getting Kids Started

The key assumptions of economics may be stated variously and applied with various emphases, depending on the grade level of the students and other circumstances that bear on teachers' instructional planning. Many curriculum publications of the National Council on Economic Education have used a formulation called the *Handy Dandy Guide for Solving Economic Mysteries* to introduce economic concepts and principles of the sort presented in the *Standards*. The *Handy Dandy Guide* can not do students' thinking for them, but it provides students with a place to begin: a source of hunches to play out against the evidence, and a means of sorting the useful clues out from the useless ones.

Here is one version of the *Handy Dandy Guide*, intended for use with upper-elementary and middle-school students. It is followed by a mystery—the Mystery of the Greedy Teenagers—which we discuss in order to illustrate the uses of the *Handy Dandy Guide* in economic reasoning.

The Handy Dandy Guide

1. People *choose* to do the things they think are best for them.
2. People's choices have *costs*.
3. People choose to do things for which they are *rewarded*.
4. People create *rules* that affect our choices and how we act.
5. People gain when they freely decide to *trade* with one another.
6. People's choices today have *future* results.

The Mystery of the Greedy Teenagers

The mystery in this case has to do with teenage babysitters and why parents can't find enough of them:

In the United States there are about 37 million young people between the ages of 10 and 19. People from this age group are the ones most likely to work as babysitters. Yet parents in many neighborhoods today have a hard time finding babysitters. When they are lucky enough to find one, the sitter often charges high prices—sometimes from $6 to $10 an hour. The minimum wage is only $5.15 an hour! Why are today's teenage babysitters so greedy? Who do they think they are?

Is the greed explanation a good one here? Let's work through the *Handy Dandy Guide* and see what light it sheds on this mystery.

1. People *choose* to do the things they think are best for them.

This principle may seem merely to state the obvious, but stop and think for a minute about how often you hear people claim that, in one situation or another, they had no choice in the course of action they took. Sometimes the claim about not having a choice helps people to explain their behavior in a manner aimed at avoiding offense or discourtesy. Imagine, for example, that your colleagues have asked you to meet them at a favorite spot after work. You decline, saying that you can't do it tonight; your spouse is expecting you for an early dinner, so you have to get right home. While your response here

is courteous and likely to be accepted by your friends, it isn't exactly accurate. You *could* choose not to get home promptly. Under some circumstances—you witness an auto accident, for example, and spend time after the accident providing the police with an account of what you saw—you probably *would* choose not to. But tonight you'd rather get home promptly than spend time hanging out with your colleagues. Stating the point in that way, however, highlights the choice you've made to put your pals in second place. That seems a bit blunt, so you say you *have* to go home; you have *no choice*.

In these matters, young people and adults are much alike. Both are prone to deny that they are making choices in certain cases when that is exactly what they are doing. Both are prone to explain their action in these cases as a matter of necessity—perhaps one imposed by others. Consider, for example, a student who comes late to class and says that he couldn't help it; he missed the bus, or the bus was late, so he had to come late. But the *Handy Dandy Guide* invites us to consider that the student in this case *chooses* to be late. Seem ridiculous? An unfamiliar line of thinking, perhaps, but not ridiculous. The student *could* have done things to get himself to class on time. He could have taken an earlier bus—just in case—or insisted that his parents get up at the crack of dawn to drive him to school early. He *could* have requested permission to sleep over in the classroom!

Not likely, you say. True enough, but likelihood is not the point here. The student did in fact have choices, and the choice he settled for got him to school late. If on-time arrival at school had been much more important to him than it actually was, he would have made the decisions necessary to insure an on-time arrival. How many students would miss a bus if missing it meant staying longer in school or losing an opportunity to meet a favorite athlete or celebrity?

What does this have to do with teenage babysitters? Teenagers who could work as babysitters make choices about whether to accept babysitting jobs or not. Many of them apparently think that the costs of babysitting are not worth the benefits.

2. People's choices have *costs*.

Decisions come with costs. Always. This is clear enough in the case of decisions to buy something. But the costs that come with decisions aren't always dollar costs. Decide to linger a while at the beach, watching a sunset, and your cost might be, for example, missing a phone call back home. You might count it a good bargain, but that's just another way of saying that missing the phone call was a cost you were willing to pay.

While there are many types of costs, economists stress the importance of opportunity costs. In the case of any decision, the opportunity cost is an individual's second-best choice. It is the road not taken, the alternative not selected. It is not *every* alternative not selected, however. After all, the list of possible alternatives in a given case is endless. The woman who lingered at the beach to watch the sunset could have hurried home to be there for the phone call, or she could have gone off to the library, or she could have gotten the oil changed in her car, or she could have. . . . Of all these possibilities, her opportunity cost is the most-valued or second best alternative that she didn't select.

When teenagers choose to accept a baby-sitting job, they pay an opportunity cost. That cost is the next-best alternative they give up in order to take the sitter's job. For one teenager, it might be an evening of soccer practice. For another, it might be homework. For another, an evening's work at a higher-paying job. Teenagers who decline to work as sitters apparently aren't willing to pay opportunity costs of this sort.

3. People choose to do things for which they are *rewarded*.

Rewards or incentives are the key to solving nearly every economic mystery. Economist Steven Landsburg writes in *The Armchair Economist* that "most of economics can be summarized in four words: people respond to incentives. The rest is commentary."

One powerful incentive is money. It is a powerful incentive because it can be exchanged for many other things people desire. It can be used now or saved for future use, spent to paint the town red or invested in a college education, given to charity or saved for retirement. No wonder most people prefer to have more money rather than less. But knowing this about people reveals little to nothing about anybody's character, since people with money may use it wisely or foolishly, on themselves or on others. All we know for sure about the appeal of money, therefore, is that it is widespread.

Not all incentives are monetary, of course. People often perform acts of kindness that involve no material reward. They find satisfaction in knowing they did the right thing. Or people vote on election day or perform volunteer services at a homeless shelter, again for no material reward. They do so, perhaps, to fulfill a sense of duty or obligation. In one sense, however, even behavior of this sort is explained by economic principles; it reflects self-interest, economists say, not selfishness. The self-interest in question is interest in the satisfaction or peace of mind gained through kindness, generosity, and so on.

Do teachers respond to incentives? Many people observe that teachers do their work for relatively low salaries. Therefore, some say, teachers do not respond much to incentives; their motivation is different. Let's examine this argument. A key incentive for primary-grade teachers is the satisfaction they gain in watching their students learn to read. These teachers may become irritated when interruptions—school announcements in the middle of class, for example—get in the way of their teaching. Why the anger? Because the interruptions diminish, at least for the moment, the satisfaction that comes with seeing children learn.

How do incentives bear on the case of teenagers who choose not to babysit? These teenagers must be responding to incentives other than those attached to babysitting. Young women, for example, now have more opportunities than their mothers had to participate in after-school sports. Young women and young men who want salaried after-school jobs often succeed in finding them. In this climate of expanded opportunities, the cost of babysitting has gone up for teenagers—the opportunity cost, that is. In order to hire babysitters, then, parents must offer pay rates and perks—pizza and videos, perhaps—adequate to compensate teenagers for the opportunity costs created by a host of new incentives.

4. People create *rules* that affect our choices and how we act.

Economic behavior occurs in a climate of rules, formal and informal. The "rules of the game" influence the choices people make in particular cases. Tax laws, for example, influence people's behavior. If a municipal government places a high tax on the width of new buildings, tall and narrow buildings soon begin popping up. If a state government places a large tax on savings accounts, people soon begin keeping less money in their passbook accounts.

How might the "rules of the game" affect teenage babysitting? While many young people do hold jobs, child labor laws restrict their work hours and the types of work they may legally perform. Older teenagers are generally granted more latitude in the job market, and their jobs often pay better than babysitting. This puts pressure on parents to compete for the services of younger teenagers, who may not be permitted to work in retail stores and fast food restaurants.

5. People gain when they freely decide to *trade* with one another.

Economists have discovered that voluntary or free trade creates wealth.

"Voluntary" here refers to a lack of coercion. "Your money or your life!" does not describe an instance of voluntary trade. "Wealth" refers to money, of course, but also to other benefits: When

Thelma drives Louise to the airport and borrows Louise's car while Louise is away, both parties may feel better off as a result. Thelma gets the use of a car, and Louise gets her car attended to during her absence. Examples of voluntary trade are everywhere. Purchasing a movie ticket, filling a car with gas, trading paperback books—all involve voluntary trade in which something is exchanged for something else.

The discovery about voluntary trade implies also an opposing proposition that is equally instructive. Involuntary trade decreases wealth, leaving behind only the victors and the vanquished, not a satisfied set of trading partners. Involuntary trade, imposed by one party through the use of force or a threat to use force, differs little from a heist, a theft, a mugging. Slavery in the United States provides a vivid example from our past. Slave traders sold Africans to people who forced them to work, under threat of severe punishment for noncompliance. The harmful legacy of that system, in which the participation of enslaved Africans was obtained only by coercion, is one from which the United States has yet to recover.

What does voluntary trade have to do with babysitting? The couple next-door cannot force teenagers to sit for them. They can only make offers to potential babysitters, in an effort to prompt voluntary trade. Parents who succeed in finding a babysitter will therefore be those offering a sufficient incentive. When this happens, we surmise that both sides gain from the exchange. The parents gain a night together for dinner and a movie. The babysitter gains the promise of payment plus perks—the ubiquitous video and pizza, or perhaps uninterrupted use of the telephone.

Things can go wrong, of course. Because both sides *think* they will gain through voluntary trade does not insure that they *will* gain in fact. The kids could turn out to be terrible brats, so that sitting for them at the agreed-upon rate turns out to be a bad bargain. The sitter could turn out to be irresponsible—spending the evening watching XXX videos, ignoring the kids, and snuffing out cigarettes in the potted plants, so that hiring her or him at the agreed-upon rate turns out to be a bad bargain. In such cases of unsatisfied expectations, the transaction is not likely to be repeated. It would most likely not have occurred in the first place if the participants in question had had the benefit of better information.

6. People's choices today have *future* results.

Despite certain messages conveyed by advertisements and quack therapists, people seldom "live for today." More often, people "live for tomorrow"—or they live, at least, with some thought of tomorrow tucked away in the backs of their minds. We keep our houses painted because the fresh paint looks good, but we know, too, that a coat of paint now may cut down on maintenance costs later. We read a book for pleasure, but we know, too, that we have been hurrying around too much lately, and we might feel better if we set time aside once in a while to sit still and relax.

Teachers routinely report that inservice workshops are notorious for their poor quality. So why do teachers attend them? They are paid to attend them, of course, and future benefits accrue to employees who do what they are paid to do. Also, hope springs eternal: perhaps this *next* inservice will be the one that really does convey useful knowledge. Here, too, the expectation of future benefits provides the criterion for choice.

Similarly, parties to the babysitting transaction are likely to be mindful of decisions and consequences that may follow some time in the future. If parents have found a responsible babysitter at what seems to be a fair price, given the competition, their immediate experience may influence their decisions about whom to call the next time they decide to go out. The immediate experience might alert them also to the possibility that this sitter could be hired for other, more responsible child-care or household jobs in the future. The babysitter may have his or her eye on the future, too. One job now might pave the way for babysitting jobs later with other par-

ents—perhaps even for summer employment—and for good recommendations for other jobs.

The Mystery in Retrospect: What's Greed Got to Do with It?

We have discussed the babysitting example at some length in order to introduce the *Handy Dandy Guide* and to illustrate its uses as a prompt in tasks of economic reasoning. With practice, students can learn to use the *HDG* in ways that lead them to new insights about the curiosities and anomalies in our world that seem to cry out for explanation. The chapters that follow are intended to help teachers provide the necessary practice. Before moving on, however, let us reconsider the mystery with which we began.

Why do parents in many neighborhoods today have a hard time finding babysitters? Are today's teenagers a greedy, money-grubbing lot, compared to their predecessors? Our analysis, aided by the *Handy Dandy Guide*, suggests that teenagers and parents are in a new situation today, and that greed has little to do with the pay and the perks paid to babysitters. Young people today have many possible uses for their time; the decisions they make invariably involve considerations of cost. In order to gain a teenager's voluntary cooperation, parents must provide an attractive incentive: adequate pay and perks. The dollar amounts in question may look high in a given case, but the underlying explanation involves incentives and choices, not greed.

CHAPTER 2

Using the Mysteries: A Teacher's Guide

The Focus on Mysteries

The lessons that follow focus on mysteries—on situations or events in which something seems to be at odds with our sense of what ordinary experience and good judgment would suggest under the circumstances. The students' task is to think the mysteries through and to propose explanations for them. In working at this task, students make use of a set of economic principles—the *Handy Dandy Guide*—and some background information provided by various clues offered in the lessons. The goal is to develop students' capacity for economic reasoning.

In Chapter 1 we introduced the *Handy Dandy Guide* by discussing its relevance to the Mystery of the Greedy Teenagers. Here we'll suggest some general ideas to help you get started working with mysteries of this sort. But first we provide another example of a mystery—one quite different from the babysitting mystery—in order to suggest the wide range of possibilities to which our suggested line of practice may be applied.

The Mystery of the Resourceful Shoppers

In a certain country in the Caribbean, low-income citizens visit upscale restaurants in the evening and order meals for their families. But instead of sitting down in the restaurant to enjoy the meals they have ordered, they package those meals up and take them home. This seems odd. Why would people who don't have a lot of money use restaurants as a source of carry-out food? Wouldn't it be cheaper to buy groceries in bulk and do one's own cooking, at home?

You would think so. Either the restaurant habitues are behaving irrationally, therefore, or their choice in this matter is being influenced by something that isn't immediately obvious. We know that the rules of the game can change the incentives that affect people's choices. Could this idea provide a clue? Suppose that the government in question had decided to subsidize restaurants in order to hold restaurant prices down, thus attracting tourists from the United States and Europe. Suppose further that the same government had pursued economic policies at home that created severe shortages of basic foodstuffs, thus driving grocery prices sky high. Under these circumstances, even low-income people might find it cheaper to buy grilled grouper in a restaurant than to shop for rice and beans at the local market. What seemed odd on the face of it might then come into view as a case of rational choice.

Getting Started

Whether the topic is greedy teenagers or resourceful shoppers, your basic teaching task is to engage students in reasoning about the mystery. In approaching this task you will no doubt devise variations—the possibilities are ample—according to your particular classroom circumstances. Meanwhile, here are some suggestions for getting started.

1. Work with the whole class in introducing the first mystery. Select the mystery carefully for interest value and ease of understanding, so that your students get off to a good start. (The Eyeglasses Mystery often works well for this purpose.) Use an overhead projector to display the mystery on a screen, if you can, and read the projected mystery aloud, clarifying it as necessary. Then invite the class to speculate on possible explanations. Almost nothing is too outrageous at this point.

2. Display the *Handy Dandy Guide*. (A big wall chart may suit this purpose well, since the *HDG* is something you'll want to refer to frequently. And your students do not need to memorize the points of the *HDG*; chemistry students, after all, do not memorize the periodic table of elements.)

Explain the meaning of each of the principles briefly and walk your students through an application of those principles to the mystery you have selected. (See the Mystery of the Greedy Teenagers in Chapter 1 as an example.) This initial presentation often results in lively discussion.

3. Read the solution to the mystery provided in the *Teachers' Guide* later in this chapter. Then revisit the *Handy Dandy Guide,* highlighting the principles that provide the most help in thinking this mystery through. While all six principles may have a bearing on the mystery, some usually provide more help than others. Encourage your students to develop arguments for the principles they find especially helpful in given cases.

4. When you are satisfied that your students have caught on to the task, introduce a new economic mystery and provide the students with the corresponding Activity sheet. Divide the class into groups and get them working on the new mystery. Remind them to use the *Handy Dandy Guide* and the true/false clues provided.

5. After an appropriate period for deliberation (brief and sharply focused is better than drawn out and meandering), ask the students in each group to settle on a consensus solution. They should record each solution, along with a brief explanation referenced to the *Handy Dandy Guide* and the clues, on the Activity sheets provided.

6. Reconvene the class as a whole group. Ask a student from each group to report the group's solution to the mystery. Then read the solution provided in the *Teachers' Guide* (see pp. 9-18) and compare it with those proposed by the groups, discussing strengths and weaknesses of each in light of the *Handy Dandy Guide* and the clues.

A Daily Lesson Plan for Elementary and Middle School Grades

For accomplishing some tasks, there are fail-safe procedures—algorithms, as mathematicians say. For paginating a manuscript, for example, you could follow an algorithm of this sort: "Put a '1' on the first page, a '2' on the second page, . . ." and so on. *Practicing* such tasks isn't very important; what counts is following the procedure correctly.

The principles of the *Handy Dandy Guide* are not algorithms. They do not provide fail-safe procedures. Instead, they provide speculative instruments, and they can be used well or poorly. *Practice* in using them is therefore very important. In order to gain fluency, flexibility, and boldness in economic reasoning, students need sustained practice in using the *HDG* principles across a wide range of applications.

As a framework for follow-up instruction aimed at providing sustained practice, we suggest the following lesson plan format.

Objectives
1. Students focus on a mystery, identifying what seems odd or unlikely in the situation in question.

2. Students examine clues and review the *Handy Dandy Guide* to decide which economic principles will be most useful in solving a given mystery.

3. Students apply one or more of the *HDG* principles to reason out a solution to a mystery.

Time Estimate
• 15-30 minutes

Materials
• One transparency of the Visual for use in presenting the mystery.

• For each student, one copy of the Activity sheet presenting the clues and the *Handy Dandy Guide.*

Lesson Description
Students describe an economic mystery and discuss various explanations of it. They use economic principles and true/false clues in reasoning out a solution to the mystery.

Procedure
1. State the purpose of the lesson: The students will use principles from the *Handy Dandy Guide* in an effort to solve an economic mystery.

2. Display the mystery on the Visual. Read the mystery aloud and clarify it as necessary. Invite the students to speculate on possible explanations.

3. Distribute the Activity sheet to the class. Review the points of the *Handy Dandy Guide* as necessary.

4. Ask the students to respond to the true/false clues, working individually or in small groups. The students will use their prior knowledge and judgment in responding. This is one reason why the use of groups can be advantageous. As necessary, circulate among the groups to offer hints and encouragement.

5. Ask the students in each group to settle on a consensus solution to the mystery, along with a brief explanation linked to the clues and one or more points of the *Handy Dandy Guide*. Each student should record the solution and explanation on his or her Activity sheet.

6. Discuss the true/false clues with the class. Refer to the *Teachers' Guide* (see pp. 9-18) for the correct answers.

7. Ask somebody from each group to present the group's solution to the mystery. Read the solution offered in the *Teachers' Guide*.

Closure
Review the mystery and the solution, discussing it and the solutions proposed by your students in light of the clues and the *Handy Dandy Guide*.

Teachers' Guide for Chapter 3
LESSON 1
The Eye Glasses Mystery
Sight is one of our most precious gifts. It helps us to do nearly everything better, including schoolwork.

Jamie is a fifth grader. He has poor eyesight. His doctor prescribed eyeglasses for him so that he would be able to see things clearly. Jamie's mother bought him a very nice pair of glasses. They fit just right, and everyone in Jamie's family said they looked great on him. They worked well, too. However, as soon as Jamie got to school, he took his glasses off and hid them in his desk. During the rest of the day Jamie never could read what the teacher wrote on the board. He had a hard time reading his textbooks, too.

Why wouldn't Jamie wear his glasses when he knew that he should?

Answers to the True or False Clues

1. Jamie enjoyed not seeing what the teacher wrote on the board. (False)
2. Looking "normal" is a reward for many people—something they would like to have. (True)
3. Many people like Jamie worry about how they look to their friends. (True)

Solution and Explanation
To Jamie, the cost of wearing eyeglasses (looking different) was not worth the reward of being able to see the assignments on the board.

While several *Handy Dandy Guide* principles apply here, the solution as stated draws primarily on principles 1, 2, and 3. (Just for fun, discuss why Jamie's parents might look at the problem differently. They probably would see Jamie's learning well in school as a reward. And while the parents pay the dollar cost of the eyeglasses, they do not pay the cost of "looking funny.")

LESSON 2
Why Stay up Late When It Wipes You Out the Next Day?

Cassandra sometimes likes to stay up late on school nights. Her father has told Cassandra that when she stays up late she wakes up crabby in the morning. Besides that, Cassandra knows that staying up late causes her to fall asleep in school the next day. Nonetheless, when there is a late TV show that Cassandra wants to watch or when she is at the end of a really good book, she stays up late after her parents fall asleep.

Why would Cassandra stay up late when she knows it will make her crabby and cause her trouble in school the next day?

Answers to the True or False Clues
1. Cassandra likes to stay up late. She sees it as a good thing to do. (True)
2. Cassandra is happy and a good student when she stays up late. (False)
3. Cassandra is not very bright. She forgets that staying up late makes her crabby and hurts her work at school. (False)

Solution and Explanation
To Cassandra, the cost of staying up late (being crabby and not doing well in school on some days) is worth the benefits she gains—finishing a good book or watching a good TV show, for example.

While several *Handy Dandy Guide* principles apply here, the solution as stated draws primarily on principles 1, 2 and 3. (Just for fun, discuss why Cassandra's parents might look at the problem differently. They probably would see Cassandra's doing well in school as a reward. And they would gain nothing from Cassandra's nighthawk behavior.)

LESSON 3
The Mystery of the Lost and Found That's Always Well Stocked

Winter in Montana is often difficult. The wind howls out of the northwest. The temperature falls below zero. The roads get icy. Snow drifts sometimes reach as high as house windows.

But in the "lost and found" cabinet of a typical elementary school in Montana, items of lost clothing pile up every day during the winter. The lost items include hats, gloves, mittens and scarves—exactly the clothing that kids need to keep warm.

Why do warm clothes go unclaimed when it is so cold outside?

Answers to the True or False Clues
1. Kids enjoy being cold. (False)
2. Parents buy clothing to keep kids warm. (True)
3. Parents always buy clothes that kids want to wear. (False)
4. Having clothes that you like to wear is like a reward. (True)
5. While kids "own" their outdoor clothing, they rarely pay for it. (True)

Solution and Explanation
Many children choose not to take good care of their outdoor clothing. They rarely pay for this clothing. And, since parents sometimes buy clothing that young people think is not attractive, the children might feel that they "gain" by losing it; they would rather freeze than look funny to their friends. The cost of losing some outdoor clothing (getting cold and risking parental disapproval) is worth the reward of not looking funny among friends—especially when the decision costs the child no money.

While several *Handy Dandy Guide* principles apply here, the solution as stated draws primarily on principles 1, 2 and 3. (Just for fun, discuss with the students why parents disapprove when children lose outdoor clothing. Parents bear direct costs, like paying for the clothing, and indirect costs, like being worried and missing work when a child comes home sick with an ailment made worse by exposure to bad weather. How might the situation be different if kids had to pay for their outdoor clothing?)

LESSON 4
The Homework Mystery

Everyone knows that doing homework helps students learn better in school and get better grades. But Louisa consistently refuses to do her homework. She says she wants to earn good grades in school; still, she never turns in her homework on time. Her teacher wants Louisa to learn, but she can't do Louisa's homework for her.

Why does Louisa not do her homework when she knows that doing it would help her get better grades?

Answers to the True or False Clues
1. Louisa likes not doing well in school. (False)
2. Students like Louisa have nothing to do after school—no chance to watch TV or play video games or play with their friends. (False)
3. Doing homework seems more like a punishment than a reward. (True)
4. Watching TV seems more like a reward than a punishment. (True)

Solution and Explanation
To Louisa, the cost of not doing homework is worth the reward of being able to do other things with her time.

While several *Handy Dandy Guide* principles apply here, the solution as stated draws primarily on principles 1, 2 and 3. (Just for fun, discuss with the students how the rewards in question might be restructured to encourage doing more homework. What might happen, for example, if Louisa could not move from grade five to grade six if she failed to complete her assignments? How might this action reorder the value she attaches to television viewing?)

LESSON 5
Could Buying Trees at Christmas Be Forest-friendly?

Every year during the winter holiday season, some environmentalists say that people who celebrate Christmas should buy artificial Christmas trees rather real spruce trees, balsams, or pines. They think that shifting over to artificial trees would save real trees from being cut down. Then we would have more trees in our wood lots and forests.

You live in a state that has many Christmas tree farms. An environmental group has proposed that all Christmas trees sold in the state must be artificial. Grizzly Jack Crosscut objects to this proposal. "If you're a friend of the forests," he says, "buy a spruce tree, a balsam, or a pine at Christmas time."

Could Grizzly Jack be right? What would happen if people were not permitted to buy or sell real trees at Christmas time?

Answers to the True or False Clues
1. Many families choose to purchase real Christmas trees. (True)
2. Christmas tree farmers produce many thousands of Christmas trees every year. (True)
3. Land used to grow Christmas trees has no other use. (False)
4. Christmas tree farmers grow Christmas trees because they are required to do so. (False)
5. Christmas trees cannot be traded or exchanged. (False)
6. Christmas trees are planted by farmers who hope to sell the trees in the future. (True)

Solution and Explanation
Grizzly Jack could be right. If people could not buy and sell real trees at Christmas time, your state would soon have fewer trees. Profits (the money left after all the expenses have been paid) are rewards tree farmers hope to earn by growing Christmas trees and selling them. The new rule prohibiting the sale of real trees would take away the rewards farmers hope to gain by growing and selling trees. It would create an incentive for them to use their farmland for other things, or perhaps to sell it to a developer in the future.

This solution draws on all six *Handy Dandy Guide* principles.

LESSON 6
What Genius Figured Out How to Get Food from the Farms to the Markets?

Whether we live in urban or rural communities, all of us need food. Farmers in rural communities produce tons of corn, beans, potatoes, milk, and meat for use by people in our community and by people around the world. As important as farming is, however, there are few rules that tell farmers how to move their products from farm to market.

How can we count on having food for our dinner tables when no one tells farmers how to get their products to the markets where we shop?

Answers to the True or False Clues

1. People in our community choose to buy food. (True)
2. Farmers can use their land for many things. (True)
3. Farmers are not allowed to keep the money they earn by selling food. (False)
4. Keeping money that you earn is a reward. (True)
5. People who own businesses in which food from farms is processed (dairies, for example) can keep the money they earn. (True)
6. Farmers keep all the food they grow; they can not trade it. (False)

Solution and Explanation

As important as farming is, there are few rules that tell farmers how to move their products from farm to market. Instead, we depend on a different kind of rule. A rule in the United States is that people can keep the profits (the money left after all the expenses have been paid) they earn from their business activity. Farmers get rewards—profits—by growing and selling food in markets. Because their rewards depend on it, farmers figure out how best to trade their products to others. If they could not earn a profit, they would eventually put their farmland to other uses.

This solution draws on all six *Handy Dandy Guide* principles.

LESSON 7
The Mystery of the Alien Bananas

Bananas are a tropical fruit. Yet they arrive in our stores all year round, even though no one in our community grows them.

How can this be? Why can we eat bananas all year round?

Answers to the True or False Clues

1. People in our community choose to buy bananas throughout the year. (True)
2. It is impossible to grow bananas in our community. (False. Yes, false is the correct answer here. People in your community *could* grow bananas indoors, no matter where you live. It would cost a lot to do this, and consumers probably would not buy bananas at the high prices that would be required by this means of production. But it still would be possible to grow the bananas indoors.)
3. Only people in Central America know how to grow bananas. (False)
4. Growers in Central America are rewarded for growing bananas. (True)
5. Shippers are paid to transport bananas from Central America to our community. (True)
6. The countries of Central America have rules that say it is okay to ship bananas to people in other countries. (True)
7. People in our community do not wish to buy food grown in other countries; it may be unhealthy. (False)

Solution and Explanation

People choose to buy bananas throughout the year. They are willing to pay for bananas (but not for bananas grown locally in greenhouses). The price grocery shoppers will pay for bananas serves as an incentive for Central American banana farmers and shippers. They are able to make a profit by selling bananas to people in other places. They find ways to grow and ship bananas to people throughout the world, all year round.

This solution draws on *Handy Dandy Guide* principles 1, 2, 3, 4, and 5.

LESSON 8
The Mystery of the Wasted Food

Every day before lunchtime, Gracie feels very hungry. When the lunch bell finally rings, Gracie hurries to the school lunchroom, grabs a tray, gets in line, receives her lunch, and finds a seat.

But before long, Gracie tosses most of her food into a waste container.

Why would hungry kids like Gracie throw away their food?

Answers to the True or False Clues
1. Gracie hates to eat. (False)
2. American students enjoy wasting food. (False)
3. The food in the cafeteria is often not popular with students. Eating it seems more like a punishment than a reward. (True)
4. School cafeterias usually offer a wide range of choices from which students may choose what they like. (False)
5. Students usually pay for their school lunches with money from their allowance or money they earn by doing work around home. (False)

Solution and Explanation

Why do students who are often ravenously hungry toss away food at school? Probably because they don't like the way it tastes. Choking down food that doesn't taste good is nobody's idea of a reward. Serving up food that doesn't taste good—at least not to the youthful palate—encourages students to make wasteful choices. It is also relevant to consider who pays for the food. Students seldom do. Government rules prohibit students from paying in some cases, while family and school traditions discourage it in other cases. There are some good reasons for these rules and traditions, but there is also an unintended consequence. When students don't pay for the food that is served to them in school, they may treat it as if it were really "free." If students bought their own lunches, using money they had earned, they would be less likely to waste it.

While several *Handy Dandy Guide* principles apply here, the solution as stated draws primarily on principles 1, 2, 3, and 4.

LESSON 9
Why Do the Cups Disappear from Room 103?

The 25 students in room 103 are a great group. They cooperate with Ms. Jackson, their teacher, they never run in the halls, and they treat one another with courtesy. Conscious of the environment, they recycle all their paper.

Four weeks ago, when the drinking fountain for the class went haywire, Ms. Jackson provided plastic cups so that the students could get drinks of water from the nearby restroom. Since then, on average, the students have used 200 plastic cups per week!

Why would a class of 25 environmentally friendly kids use up so many plastic cups?

Answers to the True or False Clues
1. Ms. Jackson's class learned how to do a magic trick—making plastic cups disappear. (False)
2. The students in Room 103 are thoughtless about the environment. (False)
3. The students owned the cups Ms. Jackson bought. (False)
4. Owning things is like a reward. (True)
5. Ms. Jackson's cups were "free" to the students. (True)

Solution and Explanation

Why do devoted recyclers overuse plastic cups? The students in Ms. Jackson's class saw little benefit in looking after the plastic cups. No one owned them. Since no one owned the cups, no one gained any benefit by taking care of them and no one seemed to suffer any loss when cups got tossed out. To Ms. Jackson's students, in other words, the cups were free. As compared with saving cups, it was easier for students to get a fresh cup each time they wanted one. Different rules—assigning each student his or her own cup, for example—might have created an incentive for students to be more responsible in their use of cups.

While several *Handy Dandy Guide* principles apply here, the solution as stated draws primarily on principles 1, 2, 3, and 4.

LESSON 10
Sherri Rejects a Sure Thing
Sherri Thompson received a special birthday gift of $2,000 from her grandmother. Sherri said she might use the money to buy some stocks. Her little brother Robert told Sherri she was crazy. "You've got $2,000 now," he said. "It's a sure thing. But if you buy stock, the stock could lose value, and then you'd wind up with less than $2,000. In fact, you could wind up with zilch. Don't be a chump, Sherri. Stash the money under your mattress."

After listening to Robert, Sherri bought 120 shares of stock.

Why would Sherri buy stock with her money? Why would she risk losing a sure thing?

Answers to the True or False Clues
1. Sherri could lose some or all of her money by buying stock with it. (True)
2. The chance to earn more money is a reward. (True)
3. Some stocks increase in value. (True)
4. Our government does not permit people to buy and keep stocks. It is too risky. (False)

Solution and Explanation
Stocks are shares of ownership in a company. Most often, they gain value after you buy them. But stocks can lose value, too. People like Sherri think that the chance to earn more money by buying a stock is worth the risk of loss. Our government permits people to make their own decisions about buying or selling stocks (within a certain set of rules).

While several *Handy Dandy Guide* principles apply here, the solution as stated draws primarily on principles 1, 2, 3, and 4.

LESSON 11
How Can You Have Sea Shells When You Don't Live By The Sea?
The Choctaw people raised plenty of corn—more than they could eat themselves. They lived along three major rivers in an area we know today as Mississippi, western Alabama, and eastern Louisiana. Yet the Choctaw had many things that came from other places. They had salt and sea shells from the sea. They had buffalo skins long after the forest buffalo in their area were gone. They also had beaver and muskrat furs from the West. And they had metal tools, metal cooking vessels, rifles, and cotton cloth from Europe.

How could Choctaw farmers obtain things they did not make—things from far away?

Answers to the True or False Clues
1. The Choctaw people chose to farm. (True)
2. The Choctaw people could raise more corn than they needed. (True)
3. The Choctaw villages were located along three major rivers. (True)
4. Other Native Americans and Europeans had things the Choctaw people wanted. (True)
5. The Choctaw people wished to depend only on themselves in obtaining things they wanted to have. (False)

Solution and Explanation
The Choctaw people chose to trade with other Native Americans and Europeans. They specialized in growing corn that could be exchanged for things they wanted. Getting things that help make your life better—like improved tools and better food—is a reward. While the Choctaw people depended on strangers to supply some things they wanted to have, their willingness to trade enabled them to live a more prosperous life.

This solution draws on *Handy Dandy Guide* principles 1, 2, 3, and 5.

LESSON 12
Why is the School Lunchroom Always Dirty?
Early in the day the school lunchroom looks spotlessly clean. But by the end of lunch you'd think the lunchroom had been hit by a tornado. Garbage piled next to (not in) the trash cans. Uneaten food scattered and smeared on table tops. Juice and milk spilled on the floor. Chairs tipped over. A first-class

mess! At home, however, the same students who trash the school lunchroom leave their dining rooms and kitchens in pretty good shape at the end of a meal.

Why is the school lunchroom trashed, while home kitchens and dining rooms are left in good shape?

Answers to the True or False Clues
1. The cooks and custodians like it when the students mess up the lunchroom. (False)
2. The school rules say that the students should leave the lunchroom a mess. (False)
3. People tend to take better care of things they own. They benefit when they take care of things they own. (True)
4. The students own the school lunchroom. (False)
5. Students and their parents own their dining rooms at home. (True. Literally true when people own their own homes and furniture. True in certain respects when people rent their living space or their furniture.)

Solution and Explanation
Students make choices about whether to keep a place messy or clean. One reason to keep a place neat and clean is that you value it or are held responsible for how you treat it. Ownership confers rewards of a sort on property owners: they stand to benefit if they take good care of the things they own. As a result, most people take better care of things they own than things they don't own. Students do not own the school lunchroom. It is probably not clear to them, in fact, who does own it—nobody they know, in any case. So they tend not to care for it as well as they care for their dining rooms at home.

This solution draws primarily on *Handy Dandy Guide* principles 1, 2, 3, and 4.

LESSON 13
Why Throw Away the Lunch Your Mom Made?
Dennis loves his mother, and she loves him. She packs a healthy lunch for him to take to school. She makes sure he has his lunch with him before she gives him a kiss goodbye. She feels good knowing Dennis will have a wholesome lunch when she can't be there with him.

At lunchtime Dennis tosses the lunch his mom made for him into the trash. He does it quietly, not making a big show of it. Dennis is really hungry by the time he gets home from school. His mother smiles, happy to know that her growing boy has a great appetite.

Why does Dennis throw away the lunch his mom makes for him?

Answers to the True or False Clues
1. Dennis hates his mom. (False)
2. Dennis' mom wants her son to grow up healthy. (True)
3. Dennis probably does not like the taste of the lunches his mom makes for him. (True)
4. Dennis pays for his own lunches. (False)

Solution and Explanation
Dennis made a choice. He decided he'd rather not hurt his mother's feelings than tell her he did not enjoy the lunches she worked so hard to prepare for him.

This solution draws primarily on *Handy Dandy Guide* principles 1, 2, and 3. (Just for fun, discuss how things might change if Dennis' mother decided that Dennis should shop for his own lunch materials and prepare his own lunches. Would he eat his lunches then? Would his lunches be nutritious? How nutritious is a lunch that is not eaten?)

LESSON 14
Why Did the English Colonies Prosper?
During colonial times, the English colonies of North America had little to offer to European settlers. There was no gold or silver for European settlers to take. There were no spices to trade.

The Spanish colonies had all the good stuff. They had vast supplies of gold and silver—treasures that seemed certain to make the Spanish colonists rich.

Yet the English colonies of North America became wealthy, while the colonies of Spain remained poor. Why did the English colonies of North America prosper?

Answers to the True or False Clues
1. Spaniards loaded gold and silver from Mexico into huge ships and sent the loot back to Spain. (True)
2. Spanish settlers were rewarded for producing new goods and services. (False)
3. English colonists in North America were allowed to keep what they earned by working their land. (True)
4. English colonists in North America were allowed to trade with Europeans—selling tobacco, for example. (True)
5. Most families in England's North American colonies owned their own farms. (True)

Solution and Explanation
The English and Spanish colonists both sought rewards of wealth, but they sought these rewards in different ways.

The Spaniards viewed gold and silver as resources that would make Spain wealthy. They chose to extract vast treasures from their colonies and ship those treasures back home to Spain. Spanish colonial authorities did little to encourage colonists to produce new goods or services. What few goods the colonists did produce were strictly controlled by the authorities. In this climate of weak incentives for production and trade, the Spanish colonies in North America experienced relatively low prosperity.

Settlers in the English colonies had no vast treasures to extract. (The California and Alaskan gold rushes came later.) It wasn't exactly clear what they should produce in their new setting. After some experimentation, they hit upon the idea of producing things that could be traded to people in Europe—tobacco, for example. English colonial authorities learned that enabling farmers to own their own land provided a reward for the farmers, encouraging them to produce goods for trade. Private property ownership and encouragement of trade helped the English colonies to prosper.

All six principles of the *Handy Dandy Guide* are important for solving this mystery. Perhaps principle 4 is the most important. The rules of the game within which colonists lived and worked in the two colonial settings affected the outcomes profoundly.

LESSON 15
Mariah Visits a Petting Zoo
The trip to a family farm was the highlight of Mariah's fourth-grade school year. Mariah and her classmates thought the farm was really great—just like a big petting zoo. The children laughed when the chickens scooted around the yard, pecking at the ground. The children loved to pet the young calves. Mariah even got to feed a baby lamb.

The class also learned about growing corn, feeding hogs, collecting eggs, caring for cattle, and stacking bales of hay.

Mariah observed that life on the farm involved a lot of work. She wondered why farmers did all this work just so kids could come to watch the animals and pet them.

Why would farmers work so hard to run a petting zoo?

Answers to the True or False Clues
1. Many students take class trips to family farms. (True)
2. Family farms are mainly big petting zoos. (False)
3. Farmers make a living producing such things as milk, meat, corn, or wheat and selling it to others. (True)
4. In order to make a living, farmers must sell enough of their products to pay all their bills and have enough left over to keep for themselves. What they have left over for themselves acts as a reward. (True)

Solution and Explanation
Farms are not petting zoos. Farms are businesses. Profits (the money left after all the expenses have been paid) are the rewards farmers hope to earn by selling what they produce. While some farmers invite school groups to visit, these visits are not the purpose of farming.

This solution draws on principles 1, 2, 3, 4, and 5 of the *Handy Dandy Guide.*

LESSON 16
The Big Piggy Bank Mystery

Sara Wilson received a $100 dollar bill as a birthday present from her grandparents. Sara's mom told her she should save her money. Sara agreed, and off they went to the bank.

Sara watched closely as the bank teller smiled and placed Sara's $100 dollar bill in the cash drawer. Sara imagined that, at the end of the day, the teller would remove Sara's $100 dollar bill from the drawer, place it an envelope marked "Sara Wilson," and place the envelope into the bank vault. Sara felt good knowing that her $100 dollar bill would be safe behind that thick vault door.

On the ride home, Sara had doubts. She asked, "Will I get the same $100 bill back when I withdraw my money from the bank?" "No, Sara," her mother explained. "You will get money back, but not the very same $100 bill your grandparents gave you. In fact, you will get more than your $100 back." Sara was shocked!

"Why won't I get my own $100 back?" asked Sara. "Isn't our family bank a safe place to keep money—sort of like a piggy bank for adults? And why would I get more money back than I put in?"

Are banks big piggy banks?

Answers to the True or False Clues
1. Many children get gifts from their grandparents. (True)
2. Bank owners keep all the money that is deposited in their banks. (False)
3. Bank owners make a living by lending money to people who want to buy a house, buy a car, or open a business. (True)
4. In order to make a living, bank owners require that people who borrow money must pay something extra back to the bank. This extra money is called interest. Interest acts as a reward for bank owners, encouraging them to lend money. (True)
5. Bank owners pay depositors some extra money because the bank owners use the deposits to make loans. The extra money is called interest. Interest is like a reward to depositors for putting their money in the bank. (True)

Solution and Explanation

Banks are not big piggy banks. Banks are businesses. Bankers pay interest to depositors to reward people like Sara who choose to put their savings into a bank. That is why Sara will receive more than her $100 back when she withdraws her savings. Profits (the money left after all the expenses have been paid) are the rewards bankers hope to earn by lending money and charging interest. In order to make a profit, bank owners must charge higher interest rates on loans than the rates they pay out to depositors.

This solution draws on principles 1, 2, 3, and 4 of the *Handy Dandy Guide.*

LESSON 17
How the People of Churchill Came to Be Fond of Polar Bears

Arctic polar bears live for most of the year on the frozen seas. But in the southern reaches of polar bear country, near Churchill, Manitoba, the bears move inland in July when the ice melts. Then in late fall they head back toward the coast of Hudson Bay. Their migratory route takes them through the town of Churchill, and as they pass through town they cause a certain amount of trouble—eating any dogs they can catch, breaking into houses to check out people's kitchens, and occasionally doing harm to people who cross their path. Until the mid-1980s, people in and around Churchill dealt with the bears by trying to avoid them and by shooting any that got close enough to be a problem.

But more recently, attitudes have changed. Polar bear hunting is now illegal in Manitoba, and the ban on bear hunting enjoys strong support in Churchill. People there have stopped shooting the bears that still traipse through town every year. In fact, they now go to great lengths to protect polar bears.

What happened? How did the people of Churchill come to be fond of polar bears?

Answers to the True or False Clues

1. Polar bears are big, carnivorous animals—on their hind legs, up to 10 feet tall. (True)
2. During polar bear migrations, people in Churchill put thick bars over their doors and windows. (True)
3. Tourists have little interest in seeing wild animals. (False)
4. When tourists visit a particular area, they spend money on motel accommodations, meals, special equipment, and souvenirs. (True)
5. Commercial outfitters now offer fall package trips to Churchill, Manitoba, including tundra-buggy outings, dog sled rides, and lectures on environmental topics. (True)

Solution and Explanation

Eco-tourism has become a big business in many parts of the world today. Many people choose to travel to remote areas in order to see wild animals in their native habitat. The tourists' interest in seeing wild animals in an authentic environment creates an incentive for people who live near those environments. It is an incentive to protect the animals and the environments. The tourists who come to see the animals also spend money in the local community, creating business opportunities and jobs for outfitters, tour guides, shop keepers, helicopter pilots, food servers, and so on. "Tundra tours" in the Churchill area now serve many eco-tourists who travel to Churchill every fall to see the migrating polar bears.

While several *Handy Dandy Guide* principles apply here, the solution as stated draws primarily in principles 3 and 5.

Mysteries for Grades Four to Eight

Chapter 3 presents the Visuals and Activity sheets you will need for lessons 1-17.

Each Visual includes one mystery, along with the *Handy Dandy Guide*. Each Activity sheet recaps the mystery and the *HDG*, for students' easy reference; each Activity sheet also presents clues and provides space in which students should write out their solutions.

Good luck!

Visual 1   The Eyeglasses Mystery

Sight is one of our most precious gifts. It helps us to do nearly everything better, including school work.

Jamie, a fifth grader, had poor eyesight. His doctor prescribed eye glasses for him so that he would be able to see things clearly. Jamie's mother bought him a very nice pair of glasses. They fit just right and everyone in Jamie's family said they looked great on him. However, as soon as Jamie got to school, he took his glasses off and hid them in his desk. During the rest of the day Jamie never could read what the teacher wrote on the board. He had a hard time reading his textbooks, too.

Why wouldn't Jamie wear his glasses when he knew that he should?

Handy Dandy Guide
1. People *choose* to do things they think are best for them.
2. People's choices have *costs*.
3. People choose to do things for which they are *rewarded*.
4. People create *rules* that affect our choices and how we act.
5. People gain when they freely decide to *trade* with one another.
6. People's choices today have *future results*.

Activity 1   The Eyeglasses Mystery

Directions. Read the *Handy Dandy Guide* and the mystery. For help in solving the mystery, read the clues and decide whether each statement is true or false. Use the ideas you get from the clues along with ideas from the *Handy Dandy Guide* to figure out a solution to the mystery. Write your solution in the space provided.

Handy Dandy Guide
1. People *choose* to do the things they think are best for them.
2. People's choices have *costs*.
3. People choose to do things for which they are *rewarded*.
4. People create *rules* that affect our choices and how we act.
5. People gain when they freely decide to *trade* with one another.
6. People's choices today have *future results*.

The Mystery
Sight is one of our most precious gifts. It helps us to do nearly everything better, including schoolwork.

Jamie, a fifth grader, had poor eyesight. His doctor prescribed eyeglasses for him so that he would be able to see things clearly. Jamie's mother bought him a very nice pair of glasses. They fit just right, and everyone in Jamie's family said they looked great on him. However, as soon as Jamie got to school, he took his glasses off and hid them in his desk. During the rest of the day Jamie never could read what the teacher wrote on the board. He had a hard time reading his textbooks, too.

Why wouldn't Jamie wear his glasses when he knew that he should?

True or False Clues
Read each statement below and mark it true (T) or false (F). Check with your teacher to find out if your responses are correct.

1. Jamie enjoyed not seeing what the teacher wrote on the board. _____
2. Looking "normal" is a reward for many people—something they'd like to have. _____
3. Many people like Jamie worry about how they look to their friends. _____

The Solution
Solve the mystery, using the clues and ideas from the *Handy Dandy Guide*. Record your solution here and explain it briefly:

_____

_____

_____

_____

Visual 2   Why Stay Up Late When You Know It Will Wipe You Out the Next Day?

Cassandra sometimes likes to stay up late on school nights. Her father has told Cassandra that when she stays up late she wakes up crabby in the morning. Besides that, Cassandra knows that staying up late causes her to fall asleep in school the next day.

Nonetheless, when there is a late TV show that Cassandra wants to watch or when she is at the end of a really good book, she stays up late after her parents fall asleep.

Why would Cassandra stay up late when she knows it will make her crabby and cause her trouble in school the next day?

Handy Dandy Guide

1. People *choose* to do the things they think are best for them.
2. People's choices have *costs*.
3. People choose to do things for which they are *rewarded*.
4. People create *rules* which affect our choices and how we act.
5. People gain when they freely decide to *trade* with one another.
6. People's choices today have *future results*.

Activity 2   Why Stay Up Late When You Know It Will Wipe You Out the Next Day?

Directions. Read the *Handy Dandy Guide* and the mystery. For help in solving the mystery, read the clues and decide whether each statement is true or false. Use the clues and ideas from the *Handy Dandy Guide* to figure out a solution to the mystery. Write your solution in the space provided.

Handy Dandy Guide

1. People *choose* to do the things they think are best for them.
2. People's choices have *costs*.
3. People choose to do things for which they are *rewarded*.
4. People create *rules* that affect our choices and how we act.
5. People gain when they freely decide to *trade* with one another.
6. People's choices today have *future results*.

The Mystery

Cassandra sometimes likes to stay up late on school nights. Her father has told Cassandra that when she stays up late she wakes up crabby in the morning. Besides that, Cassandra knows that staying up late causes her to fall asleep in school the next day. Nonetheless, when there is a late TV show that Cassandra wants to watch or when she is at the end of a really good book, she stays up late after her parents fall asleep.

Why would Cassandra stay up late when she knows it will make her crabby and cause her trouble in school the next day?

True or False Clues

Read each statement below and mark it true (T) or false (F). Check with your teacher to find out if your responses are correct.

1. Cassandra likes to stay up late. She sees it as a good thing—something she would like to do. _____
2. Cassandra is happy and a good student when she stays up late. _____
3. Cassandra is not very bright. She forgets that staying up late makes her crabby and hurts her work at school. _____

The Solution

Solve the mystery, using the clues and ideas from the *Handy Dandy Guide*. Record your solution here and explain it briefly:

_____

_____

_____

_____

Visual 3   The Mystery of the Lost and Found That's Always Well Stocked

Winter in Montana is often difficult. The wind howls out of the northwest. The temperature falls below zero. The roads get icy. Snow drifts sometimes reach as high as house windows.

But in the "lost and found" cabinet of a typical elementary school in Montana, items of lost clothing pile up every day during the winter. The lost items include hats, gloves, mittens, and scarves—exactly the clothing that kids need to keep warm.

Why do warm clothes go unclaimed when it is so cold outside?

Handy Dandy Guide
1. People *choose* to do the things they think are best for them.
2. People's choices have *costs*.
3. People choose to do things for which they are *rewarded*.
4. People create *rules* that affect our choices and how we act.
5. People gain when they freely decide to *trade* with one another.
6. People's choices today have *future results*.

Activity 3   The Mystery of the Lost and Found That's Always Well Stocked

Directions. Read the *Handy Dandy Guide* and the mystery. For help in solving the mystery, read the clues and decide whether each statement is true or false. Use the clues and ideas from the *Handy Dandy Guide* to figure out a solution to the mystery. Write your solution in the space provided.

Handy Dandy Guide
1. People *choose* to do the things they think are best for them.
2. People's choices have *costs*.
3. People choose to do things for which they are *rewarded*.
4. People create *rules* that affect our choices and how we act.
5. People gain when they freely decide to *trade* with one another.
6. People's choices today have *future results*.

The Mystery
Winter in Montana is often difficult. The wind howls out of the northwest. The temperature falls below zero. The roads get icy. Snow drifts sometimes reach as high as house windows.

But in the "lost and found" cabinet of a typical elementary school in Montana, items of lost clothing pile up every day during the winter. The lost items include hats, gloves, mittens and scarves—exactly the clothing that kids need to keep warm.

Why do warm clothes go unclaimed when it is so cold outside?

True or False Clues
Read each statement below and mark it true (T) or false (F). Check with your teacher to find out if your responses are correct.

1. Kids enjoy being cold. _____
2. Parents buy clothing to keep their kids warm. _____
3. Parents always buy clothes that kids like to wear. _____
4. Having clothes that you like to wear is like a reward. _____
5. While kids "own" their outdoor clothing, they rarely pay for it themselves. _____

The Solution
Solve the mystery, using the clues and ideas from the *Handy Dandy Guide*. Record your solution here and explain it briefly:

_____

_____

_____

_____

From *The Great Economic Mysteries Book: A Guide to Teaching Economic Reasoning Grades 4-8.* © National Council on Economic Education, New York, NY

Visual 4 The Homework Mystery

Everyone knows that doing homework helps students learn better in school and get better grades.

But Louisa consistently refuses to do her homework. She says she wants to earn good grades in school; still, she never turns in her homework on time. Her teacher wants Louisa to learn, but she can't do Louisa's homework for her.

Why does Louisa not do her homework when she knows that doing it would help her get better grades?

Handy Dandy Guide

1. People *choose* to do the things they think are best for them.
2. People's choices have *costs*.
3. People choose to do things for which they are *rewarded*.
4. People create *rules* that affect our choices and how we act.
5. People gain when they freely decide to *trade* with one another.
6. People's choices today have *future results*.

Activity 4   The Homework Mystery

Directions. Read the *Handy Dandy Guide* and the mystery. For help in solving the mystery, read the clues and decide whether each statement is true or false. Use the clues and ideas from the *Handy Dandy Guide* to figure out a solution to the mystery. Write your solution in the space provided.

Handy Dandy Guide
1. People *choose* to do the things they think are best for them.
2. People's choices have *costs*.
3. People choose to do things for which they are *rewarded*.
4. People create *rules* that affect our choices and how we act.
5. People gain when they freely decide to *trade* with one another.
6. People's choices today have *future results*.

The Mystery
Everyone knows that doing homework helps students learn better in school and get better grades. But Louisa consistently refuses to do her homework. She says she wants to earn good grades in school; still, she never turns in her homework on time. Her teacher wants Louisa to learn, but she can't do Louisa's homework for her.

Why does Louisa not do her homework when she knows that doing it would help her get better grades?

True or False Clues
Read each statement below and mark it true (T) or false (F). Check with your teacher to find out if your responses are correct.

1. Louisa likes not doing well in school. _____
2. Students like Louisa have nothing to do after school—no chance to watch TV or play video games or play with their friends. _____
3. Doing homework seems more like a punishment than a reward. _____
4. Watching TV seems more like a reward than a punishment. _____

The Solution
Solve the mystery, using the clues and ideas from the *Handy Dandy Guide.* Record your solution here and explain it briefly:

_____

_____

_____

_____

Visual 5   Could Buying Trees at Christmas Be Forest-friendly?

Every year during the winter holiday season, some environmentalists say that people who celebrate Christmas should buy artificial Christmas trees rather than spruce trees, balsams, or pines. They say that shifting over to artificial trees would save real trees from being cut down. Then we would have more trees in our wood lots and forests.

You live in a state that has many Christmas tree farms. An environmental group has proposed that all Christmas trees sold in the state must be artificial. Grizzly Jack Crosscut objects to this proposal. "If you're a friend of the forests," he says, "buy a spruce tree, a balsam, or a pine at Christmas time."

Could Grizzly Jack be right? What would happen if people were not permitted to buy and sell real trees at Christmas time?

Handy Dandy Guide
1. People *choose* to do the things they think are best for them.
2. People's choices have *costs*.
3. People choose to do things for which they are *rewarded*.
4. People create *rules* that affect our choices and how we act.
5. People gain when they freely decide to *trade* with one another.
6. People's choices today have *future results*.

Activity 5   Could Buying Trees at Christmas Be Forest-friendly?

Directions. Read the *Handy Dandy Guide* and the mystery. For help in solving the mystery, read the clues and decide whether each statement is true or false. Use the clues and ideas from the *Handy Dandy Guide* to figure out a solution to the mystery. Write your solution in the space provided.

Handy Dandy Guide

1. People *choose* to do the things they think are best for them.
2. People's choices have *costs*.
3. People choose to do things for which they are *rewarded*.
4. People create *rules* that affect our choices and how we act.
5. People gain when they freely decide to *trade* with one another.
6. People's choices today have *future results*.

The Mystery

Every year during the winter holiday season, some environmentalists say that people who celebrate Christmas should buy artificial Christmas trees rather spruce trees, balsams, or pines. They think that shifting over to artificial trees would save real trees from being cut down. Then we would have more trees in our wood lots and forests.

You live in a state that has many Christmas tree farms. An environmental group has proposed that all Christmas trees sold in the state must be artificial. Grizzly Jack Crosscut objects to this proposal. "If you're a friend of the forests," he says, "buy a spruce tree, a balsam, or a pine at Christmas time."

Could Grizzly Jack be right? What would happen if people were not permitted to buy or sell real trees at Christmas time?

True or False Clues

Read each statement below and mark it true (T) or false (F). Check with your teacher to find out if your responses are correct.

1. Many families choose to purchase real Christmas trees. _____
2. Christmas tree farmers produce many thousands of Christmas trees every year. _____
3. Land used to grow Christmas trees has no other use. _____
4. Christmas tree farmers grow Christmas trees because they are required to do so. _____
5. Christmas trees can not be traded or exchanged. _____
6. Farmers who plant and grow Christmas trees hope to sell the trees in the future. _____

The Solution

Solve the mystery, using the clues and ideas from the *Handy Dandy Guide*. Record your solution here and explain it briefly:

_____

_____

_____

_____

Visual 6   What Genius Figured Out How to Get Food from the Farms to the Markets?

Whether we live in urban or rural communities, all of us need food.   Farmers in rural communities produce tons of corn, beans, potatoes, milk, and meat for use by people in our community and around the world.

As important as farming is, however, there are few rules that tell farmers how to move their products from farm to market.

How can we count on having food for our dinner tables when no one tells farmers how to get their products to the markets?

Handy Dandy Guide
1. People *choose* to do the things they think are best for them.
2. People's choices have *costs*.
3. People choose to do things for which they are *rewarded*.
4. People create *rules* that affect our choices and how we act.
5. People gain when they freely decide to *trade* with one another.
6. People's choices today have *future results*.

Activity 6   What Genius Figured Out How to Get Food from the Farms to the Markets?

Directions.   Read the *Handy Dandy Guide* and the mystery. For help in solving the mystery, read the clues and decide whether each statement is true or false. Use the clues and ideas from the *Handy Dandy Guide* to figure out a solution to the mystery. Write your solution in the space provided.

Handy Dandy Guide
1. People *choose* to do the things they think are best for them.
2. People's choices have *costs*.
3. People choose to do things for which they are *rewarded*.
4. People create *rules* that affect our choices and how we act.
5. People gain when they freely decide to *trade* with one another.
6. People's choices today have *future results*.

The Mystery
Whether we live in urban or rural communities, all of us need food. Farmers in rural communities produce tons of corn, beans, potatoes, milk, and meat for use by people in our community and around the world. As important as farming is, however, there are few rules that tell farmers how to move their products from farm to market.

How can we count on having food for our dinner tables when no one tells farmers how to get their products to the markets where we shop?

True or False Clues
Read each statement below and mark it true (T) or false (F). Check with your teacher to find out if your responses are correct.

1. People in our community choose to buy food. _____
2. Farmers can use their land for many things. _____
3. Farmers are not allowed to keep the money they earn by selling food. _____
4. Keeping money that you earn is a reward. _____
5. People who own businesses in which food from farms is processed (dairies, for example) can keep the money they earn. _____
6. Farmers keep all the food they grow; they cannot trade it. _____

The Solution
Solve the mystery, using the clues and ideas from the *Handy Dandy Guide*. Record your solution here and explain it briefly:

_____

_____

_____

_____

Visual 7   The Mystery of the Alien Bananas

Bananas are a tropical fruit. Yet they arrive in our stores all year round, even though no one in our community grows them.

How can this be? Why can we eat bananas all year round?

Handy Dandy Guide

1. People *choose* to do the things they think are best for them.
2. People's choices have *costs*.
3. People choose to do things for which they are *rewarded*.
4. People create *rules* that affect our choices and how we act.
5. People gain when they freely decide to *trade* with one another.
6. People's choices today have *future results*.

Activity 7   The Mystery of the Alien Bananas

Directions.   Read the *Handy Dandy Guide* and the mystery. For help in solving the mystery, read the clues and decide whether each statement is true or false. Use the clues and ideas from the *Handy Dandy Guide* to figure out a solution to the mystery. Write your solution in the space provided.

Handy Dandy Guide
1. People *choose* to do the things they think are best for them.
2. People's choices have *costs*.
3. People choose to do things for which they are *rewarded*.
4. People create *rules* that affect our choices and how we act.
5. People gain when they freely decide to *trade* with one another.
6. People's choices today have *future results*.

The Mystery
Bananas are a tropical fruit. Yet they arrive in our stores all year round, even though no one in our community grows them.

How can this be? Why can we eat bananas all year round?

True or False Clues
Read each statement below and mark it true (T) or false (F). Check with your teacher to find out if your responses are correct.

1. People in our community choose to buy bananas throughout the year. _____
2. It is impossible to grow bananas in our community. _____
3. Only people in Central America know how to grow bananas. _____
4. Growers in Central America are rewarded for growing bananas. _____
5. Shippers are paid to transport bananas from Central America to our community.
6. The countries of Central America have rules that permit shipment of bananas to people in other countries. _____
7. People in our community do not wish to buy food grown by people in other countries; it may be unhealthy. _____

The Solution
Solve the mystery, using the clues and ideas from the *Handy Dandy Guide*. Record your solution here and explain it briefly:

_____

_____

_____

_____

     From *The Great Economic Mysteries Book: A Guide to Teaching Economic Reasoning Grades 4-8.* © National Council on Economic Education, New York, NY

Visual 8   The Mystery of the Wasted Food

Even before lunchtime, Gracie feels very hungry. When the bell for lunch finally rings, Gracie hurries to the school lunchroom, grabs a tray, gets in line, receives her lunch, and finds a seat.

But before long, Gracie tosses most of her food into a waste container.

Why would hungry kids like Gracie throw away their food?

Handy Dandy Guide
1. People *choose* to do the things they think are best for them.
2. People's choices have *costs*.
3. People choose to do things for which they are *rewarded*.
4. People create *rules* that affect our choices and how we act.
5. People gain when they freely decide to *trade* with one another.
6. People's choices today have *future results*.

Activity 8   The Mystery of the Wasted Food

Directions. Read the *Handy Dandy Guide* and the mystery. For help in solving the mystery, read the clues and decide whether each statement is true or false. Use the clues and ideas from the *Handy Dandy Guide* to figure out a solution to the mystery. Write your solution in the space provided.

Handy Dandy Guide
1. People *choose* to do the things they think are best for them.
2. People's choices have *costs*.
3. People choose to do things for which they are *rewarded*.
4. People create *rules* that affect our choices and how we act.
5. People gain when they freely decide to *trade* with one another.
6. People's choices today have *future results*.

The Mystery
Even before lunchtime, Gracie feels very hungry. When the lunch bell finally rings, Gracie hurries to the school lunchroom, grabs a tray, gets in line, receives her lunch, and finds a seat.

But before long, Gracie tosses most of her food into a waste container.

Why would hungry kids like Gracie throw away their food?

True or False Clues
Read each statement below and mark it true (T) or false (F). Check with your teacher to find out if your responses are correct.

1. Gracie hates to eat. _____
2. American students enjoy wasting food. _____
3. The food in the school cafeteria is often not popular with students. Eating it seems more like a punishment than a reward. _____
4. School cafeterias usually offer a wide range of choices from which students may choose what they like. _____
5. Students usually pay for their school lunches with money from their allowances or money they earn by doing work around home. _____

The Solution
Solve the mystery, using the clues and ideas from the *Handy Dandy Guide*. Record your solution here and explain it briefly:

_____

_____

_____

_____

Visual 9   Why Do the Cups Disappear from Room 103?

The 25 students in room 103 are a great group. They cooperate with Ms. Jackson, their teacher, they never run in the halls, and they treat one another with courtesy. Conscious of the environment, they recycle all their paper.

Four weeks ago, when the drinking fountain for the class went haywire, Ms. Jackson provided plastic cups so that her students could get drinks of water from the nearby restroom. Since then, on average, the students have been using 200 plastic cups per week!

Why would a class of 25 environmentally friendly kids use up so many plastic cups?

Handy Dandy Guide
1. People *choose* to do the things they think are best for them.
2. People's choices have *costs*.
3. People choose to do things for which they are *rewarded*.
4. People create *rules* that affect our choices and how we act.
5. People gain when they freely decide to *trade* with one another.
6. People's choices today have *future results*.

Activity 9   Why Do the Cups Disappear from Room 103?

Directions. Read the *Handy Dandy Guide* and the mystery. For help in solving the mystery, read the clues and decide whether each statement is true or false. Use the clues and ideas from the *Handy Dandy Guide* to figure out a solution to the mystery. Write your solution in the space provided.

Handy Dandy Guide
1. People *choose* to do the things they think are best for them.
2. People's choices have *costs*.
3. People choose to do things for which they are *rewarded*.
4. People create *rules* that affect our choices and how we act.
5. People gain when they freely decide to *trade* with one another.
6. People's choices today have *future results*.

The Mystery
The 25 students in room 103 are a great group. They cooperate with Ms. Jackson, their teacher, they never run in the halls, and they treat one another with courtesy. Conscious of the environment, they recycle all their paper.

Four weeks ago, when the drinking fountain for the class went haywire, Ms. Jackson provided plastic cups so that the students could get drinks of water from the nearby restroom. Since then, on average, the students have used 200 plastic cups per week!

Why would a class of 25 environmentally friendly kids use up so many plastic cups?

True or False Clues
Read each statement below and mark it true (T) or false (F). Check with your teacher to find out if your responses are correct.

1. Ms. Jackson's class learned how to do a magic trick: making plastic cups disappear. _____
2. The students in Room 103 are thoughtless about the environment. _____
3. The students owned the cups Ms. Jackson bought. _____
4. Owning things is like a reward. _____
5. Ms. Jackson's cups were "free" to the students. _____

The Solution
Solve the mystery, using the clues and ideas from the *Handy Dandy Guide*. Record your solution here and explain it briefly:

_____

_____

_____

_____

Visual 10   Sherri Rejects a Sure Thing

Sherri Thompson received a special birthday gift of $2,000 from her grandmother. After thinking it over, Sherri said she might use the money to buy some stocks.

Her little brother Robert told Sherri she was crazy. "You've got $2,000 now," he said. "It's a sure thing. But if you buy stocks, the stocks could lose value, and then you'd wind up with less than $2,000. In fact, you could wind up with zilch. Don't be a chump, Sherri. Stash the money under your mattress."

After listening to Robert, Sherri bought 120 shares of stock.

Why would Sherri buy stock with her money? Why would she risk losing a sure thing?

Handy Dandy Guide
1. People *choose* to do the things they think are best for them.
2. People's choices have *costs*.
3. People choose to do things for which they are *rewarded*.
4. People create *rules* that affect our choices and how we act.
5. People gain when they freely decide to *trade* with one another.
6. People's choices today have *future results*.

Activity 10   Sherri Rejects a Sure Thing

Directions.   Read the *Handy Dandy Guide* and the mystery. For help in solving the mystery, read the clues and decide whether each statement is true or false. Use the clues and ideas from the *Handy Dandy Guide* to figure out a solution to the mystery. Write your solution in the space provided.

The Mystery
Sherri Thompson received a special birthday gift of $2,000 from her grandmother. After thinking it over, Sherri said she might use the money to buy some stocks. Her little brother Robert told Sherri she was crazy. "You've got $2,000 now," he said. "It's a sure thing. But if you buy stock, the stock could lose value, and then you'd wind up with less than $2,000. In fact, you could wind up with zilch. Don't be a chump, Sherri. Stash the money under your mattress."

After listening to Robert, Sherri bought 120 shares of stock.

Why would Sherri buy stock with her money? Why would she risk losing a sure thing?

True or False Clues
Read each statement below and mark it true (T) or false (F). Check with your teacher to find out if your responses are correct.

1. Sherri could lose some or all of her money by buying stock with it. _____
2. The chance to earn more money is a reward._____
3. Some stocks increase in value. _____
4. Our government does not permit people to buy and keep stocks. It's too risky._____

The Solution
Solve the mystery, using the clues and ideas from the *Handy Dandy Guide*. Record your solution here and explain it briefly:

_____

_____

_____

_____

Visual 11   How Can You Have Sea Shells When You Don't Live by the Sea?

The Choctaw people raised plenty of corn—more than they could eat themselves. They lived along three major rivers in an area we know today as Mississippi, western Alabama, and eastern Louisiana.

Yet the Choctaw had many things that came from other places. They had salt and sea shells from the sea. They had buffalo skins long after the forest buffalo in their area were gone. They also had beaver and muskrat furs from the West. And they had metal tools, metal cooking vessels, rifles, and cotton cloth from Europe.

How could Choctaw farmers obtain things they did not make—things from far away?

Handy Dandy Guide
1. People *choose* to do the things they think are best for them.
2. People's choices have *costs*.
3. People choose to do things for which they are *rewarded*.
4. People create *rules* that affect our choices and how we act.
5. People gain when they freely decide to *trade* with one another.
6. People's choices today have *future results*.

Activity 11   How Can You Have Sea Shells When You Don't Live by the Sea?

Directions.   Read the *Handy Dandy Guide* and the mystery. For help in solving the mystery, read the clues and decide whether each statement is true or false. Use the clues and ideas from the *Handy Dandy Guide* to figure out a solution to the mystery. Write your solution in the space provided.

Handy Dandy Guide
1. People *choose* to do the things they think are best for them.
2. People's choices have *costs*.
3. People choose to do things for which they are *rewarded*.
4. People create *rules* that affect our choices and how we act.
5. People gain when they freely decide to *trade* with one another.
6. People's choices today have *future results*.

The Mystery
The Choctaw people raised plenty of corn—more than they could eat themselves. They lived along three major rivers in an area we know today as Mississippi, western Alabama, and eastern Louisiana.   Yet the Choctaw had many things that came from other places. They had salt and sea shells from the sea. They had buffalo skins long after the forest buffalo in their area were gone. They also had beaver and muskrat furs from the West. And they had metal tools, metal cooking vessels, rifles, and cotton cloth from Europe.

How could Choctaw farmers obtain things they did not make—things from far away?

True or False Clues
Read each statement below and mark it true (T) or false (F). Check with your teacher to find out if your responses are correct.

1. The Choctaw people chose to farm. _____
2. The Choctaw people could raise more corn than they needed. _____
3. The Choctaw villages were located along three major rivers. _____
4. Other Native Americans and Europeans had things the Choctaw people wanted. _____
5. The Choctaw people wished to depend only on themselves to obtain the things they wanted. _____

The Solution
Solve the mystery, using the clues and ideas from the *Handy Dandy Guide*. Record your solution here and explain it briefly:

_____

_____

_____

_____

   From *The Great Economic Mysteries Book: A Guide to Teaching Economic Reasoning Grades 4-8.* © National Council on Economic Education, New York, NY

Visual 12   Why is the School Lunchroom Always Dirty?

Early in the day, the school lunchroom looks spotlessly clean. But by the end of lunch you'd think the lunchroom had been hit by a tornado. Garbage tossed next to (not in) the trash cans. Uneaten food scattered and smeared on table tops. Juice and milk spilled on the floor. Chairs tipped over. A first-class mess!

At home, however, the same students who trash the school lunchroom leave their dining rooms or kitchens in pretty good shape at the end of a meal.

Why is the school lunchroom trashed, while home kitchens and dining rooms are left in good shape?

Handy Dandy Guide
1. People *choose* to do the things they think are best for them.
2. People's choices have *costs*.
3. People choose to do things for which they are *rewarded*.
4. People create *rules* that affect our choices and how we act.
5. People gain when they freely decide to *trade* with one another.
6. People's choices today have *future results*.

Activity 12 Why is the School Lunchroom Always Dirty?

Directions. Read the *Handy Dandy Guide* and the mystery. For help in solving the mystery, read the clues and decide whether each statement is true or false. Use the clues and ideas from the *Handy Dandy Guide* to figure out a solution to the mystery. Write your solution in the space provided.

Handy Dandy Guide
1. People *choose* to do the things they think are best for them.
2. People's choices have *costs*.
3. People choose to do things for which they are *rewarded*.
4. People create *rules* that affect our choices and how we act.
5. People gain when they freely decide to *trade* with one another.
6. People's choices today have *future results*.

The Mystery
Early in the day, the school lunchroom looks spotlessly clean. But by the end of lunch you'd think the lunchroom had been hit by a tornado. Garbage piled next to (not in) the trash cans. Uneaten food scattered and smeared on table tops. Juice and milk spilled on the floor. Chairs tipped over. A first-class mess! At home, however, the same students who trash the school lunchroom leave their dining rooms and kitchens in pretty good shape at the end of a meal.

Why is the school lunchroom trashed, while home kitchens and dining rooms are left in good shape?

True or False Clues
Read each statement below and mark it true (T) or false (F). Check with your teacher to find out if your responses are correct.

1. The school cooks and custodians like it when the students mess up the cafeteria. _____
2. The rules in the school say that the students should leave the lunchroom a mess. _____
3. People tend to take better care of things they own. They benefit when they take care of the things they own. _____
4. The students own the school lunchroom. _____
5. Students and their parents own their dining rooms at home. _____

The Solution
Solve the mystery, using the clues and ideas from the *Handy Dandy Guide*. Record your solution here and explain it briefly:

_____

_____

_____

_____

Visual 13   Why Throw Away the Lunch Your Mom Made?

Dennis loves his mother, and his mother loves him. She packs a healthy lunch for him to take to school. She makes sure he has his lunch with him before she gives him a kiss goodbye. She feels good knowing Dennis will have a wholesome lunch when she can't be there with him.

At lunchtime Dennis tosses the lunch his mom made for him into the trash. He does it quietly, not making a big show of it.

Dennis is really hungry by the time he gets home from school. His mother smiles, happy to know that her growing boy has a great appetite.

Why does Dennis throw away the lunch his mom makes for him?

Handy Dandy Guide
1. People *choose* to do the things they think are best for them.
2. People's choices have *costs*.
3. People choose to do things for which they are *rewarded*.
4. People create *rules* that affect our choices and how we act.
5. People gain when they freely decide to *trade* with one another.
6. People's choices today have *future results*.

Activity 13   Why Throw Away the Lunch Your Mom Made?

Directions. Read the *Handy Dandy Guide* and the mystery. For help in solving the mystery, read the clues and decide whether each statement is true or false. Use the clues and ideas from the *Handy Dandy Guide* to figure out a solution to the mystery. Write your solution in the space provided.

Handy Dandy Guide
1. People *choose* to do the things they think are best for them.
2. People's choices have *costs*.
3. People choose to do things for which they are *rewarded*.
4. People create *rules* which affect our choices and how we act.
5. People gain when they freely decide to *trade* with one another.
6. People's choices today have *future results*.

The Mystery
Dennis loves his mother, and she loves him. She packs a healthy lunch for him to take to school. She makes sure he has his lunch with him before she gives him a kiss goodbye. She feels good knowing Dennis will have a wholesome lunch when she can't be there with him.

At lunchtime Dennis tosses the lunch his mom made for him into the trash. He does it quietly, not making a big show of it. Dennis is really hungry by the time he gets home from school. His mother smiles, happy to know that her growing boy has a great appetite.

Why does Dennis throw away the lunch his mom makes for him?

True or False Clues
Read each statement below and mark it true (T) or false (F). Check with your teacher to find out if your responses are correct.

1. Dennis hates his mom. _____
2. Dennis' mom wants her son to grow up healthy. _____
3. Dennis probably does not like the taste of the lunches his mom makes for him. _____
4. Dennis pays for his own lunches. _____

The Solution
Solve the mystery, using the clues and ideas from the *Handy Dandy Guide.* Record your solution here and explain it briefly:

_____

_____

_____

_____

Visual 14   Why Did the English Colonies in North America Prosper?

During colonial times, the English colonies in North America had little to offer to European settlers. There was no gold or silver for settlers to take. There were no spices to trade.

The Spanish colonies had all the good stuff. They had vast supplies of gold and silver—treasures that seemed certain to make the Spanish colonists rich.

Yet the English colonies of North America became wealthy, while the colonies of Spain remained poor. Why did the English colonies prosper?

Handy Dandy Guide
1. People *choose* to do the things they think are best for them.
2. People's choices have *costs*.
3. People choose to do things for which they are *rewarded*.
4. People create *rules* that affect our choices and how we act.
5. People gain when they freely decide to *trade* with one another.
6. People's choices today have *future results*.

Activity 14 Why Did the English Colonies in North America Prosper?

Directions. Read the *Handy Dandy Guide* and the mystery. For help in solving the mystery, read the clues and decide whether each statement is true or false. Use the clues and ideas from the *Handy Dandy Guide* to figure out a solution to the mystery. Write your solution in the space provided.

Handy Dandy Guide
1. People *choose* to do the things they think are best for them.
2. People's choices have *costs*.
3. People choose to do things for which they are *rewarded*.
4. People create *rules* that affect our choices and how we act.
5. People gain when they freely decide to *trade* with each other.
6. People's choices today have *future results*.

The Mystery
During colonial times, the English colonies in North America had little to offer to European settlers. There was no gold or silver for settlers to take. There were no spices to trade.

The Spanish colonies had all the good stuff. They had vast supplies of gold and silver—treasures that seemed certain to make the Spanish colonists rich.

Yet the English colonies of North America became wealthy, while the colonies of Spain remained poor. Why did the English colonies of North America prosper?

True or False Clues
Read each statement below and mark it true (T) or false (F). Check with your teacher to find out if your responses are correct.

1. Spaniards loaded gold and silver from Mexico into huge ships and sent the loot home to Spain. _____
2. Spanish settlers were rewarded for making new goods and services. _____
3. English colonists in North America were allowed to keep what they earned from working their land. _____
4. English colonists in North America were allowed to trade products like tobacco to Europeans. _____
5. Most families in England's North American colonies owned their own farms. _____

The Solution
Solve the mystery, using the clues and ideas from the *Handy Dandy Guide*. Record your solution here and explain it briefly:

_____

_____

_____

_____

Visual 15 Mariah Visits a Petting Zoo

The trip to a family farm was the highlight of Mariah's fourth-grade school year. Mariah and her classmates thought the farm was really great—just like a big petting zoo. The children laughed when the chickens scooted around the yard, pecking at the ground. The children loved to pet the young calves. Mariah even got to feed a baby lamb.

The class also learned about growing corn, feeding hogs, collecting eggs, caring for cattle, and stacking bales of hay.

Mariah observed that life on the farm involved a lot of work. She wondered why farmers did all this work just so kids could come to watch the animals and pet them.

Why would farmers work so hard to run a petting zoo?

Handy Dandy Guide
1. People *choose* to do the things they think are best for them.
2. People's choices have *costs*.
3. People choose to do things for which they are *rewarded*.
4. People create *rules* that affect our choices and how we act.
5. People gain when they freely decide to *trade* with one another.
6. People's choices today have *future results*.

Activity 15   Mariah Visits a Petting Zoo

Directions. Read the *Handy Dandy Guide* and the mystery. For help in solving the mystery, read the clues and decide whether each statement is true or false. Use the clues and ideas from the *Handy Dandy Guide* to figure out a solution to the mystery. Write your solution in the space provided.

Handy Dandy Guide
1. People *choose* to do the things they think are best for them.
2. People's choices have *costs*.
3. People choose to do things for which they are *rewarded*.
4. People create *rules* that affect our choices and how we act.
5. People gain when they freely decide to *trade* with each other.
6. People's choices today have *future results*.

The Mystery
The trip to a family farm was the highlight of Mariah's fourth-grade school year. Mariah and her classmates thought the farm was really great—just like a big petting zoo. The children laughed when the chickens scooted around the yard, pecking at the ground. The children loved to pet the young calves. Mariah even got to feed a baby lamb.

The class also learned about growing corn, feeding hogs, collecting eggs, caring for cattle, and stacking bales of hay.

Mariah observed that life on the farm involved a lot of work. She wondered why farmers did all this work just so kids could come to watch the animals and pet them.

Why would farmers work so hard to run a petting zoo?

True or False Clues
Read each statement below and mark it true (T) or false (F). Check with your teacher to find out if your responses are correct.

1. Many students take class trips to family farms. _____
2. Farms are mainly big petting zoos. _____
3. Farmers make a living producing such things as milk, meat, corn, or wheat and selling it to others. _____
4. In order to make a living, farmers must sell enough of their products to pay all their bills and have enough left over to keep for themselves. The portion they have left for themselves acts as a reward. _____

The Solution
Solve the mystery, using the clues and ideas from the *Handy Dandy Guide*. Record your solution here and explain it briefly:

_____

_____

_____

_____

Visual 16 The Big Piggy Bank Mystery

Sara Wilson received a $100 dollar bill as a birthday present from her grandparents. Sara's mom told her she should save her money. Sara agreed, and off they went to the bank.

Sara watched closely as the bank teller smiled and placed Sara's $100 dollar bill in the cash drawer. Sara imagined that, at the end of the day, the teller would remove Sara's $100 dollar bill from the drawer, place it an envelope marked "Sara Wilson," and then place the envelope into the bank vault. Sara felt good knowing that her $100 dollar bill would be safe behind that thick vault door.

On the ride home, Sara had doubts. She asked, "Will I get the same $100 bill back when I withdraw my money from the bank?" "No, Sara," her mother explained. "You will get money back, but not the very same bill your grandparents gave you. In fact, you will get more than your $100 back." Sara was shocked!

"Why won't I get my own $100 bill back?" she asked. "Isn't our family bank a safe place to keep money—sort of like a piggy bank for adults? And why would I get more money back than I put in?"

Are banks big piggy banks?

Handy Dandy Guide
1. People *choose* to do the things they think are best for them.
2. People's choices have *costs*.
3. People choose to do things for which they are *rewarded*.
4. People create *rules* that affect our choices and how we act.
5. People gain when they freely decide to *trade* with one another.
6. People's choices today have *future results*.

Activity 16   The Big Piggy Bank Mystery

Directions.   Read the *Handy Dandy Guide* and the mystery. For help in solving the mystery, read the clues and decide whether each statement is true or false. Use the clues and ideas from the *Handy Dandy Guide* to figure out a solution to the mystery. Write your solution in the space provided.

Handy Dandy Guide

1. People *choose* to do the things they think are best for them.
2. People's choices have *costs*.
3. People choose to do things for which they are *rewarded*.
4. People create *rules* that affect our choices and how we act.
5. People gain when they freely decide to *trade* with each other.
6. People's choices today have *future results*.

The Mystery

Sara Wilson received a $100 dollar bill as a birthday present from her grandparents. Sara's mom told her she should save her money. Sara agreed, and off they went to the bank.

Sara watched closely as the bank teller smiled and placed Sara's $100 dollar bill in the cash drawer. Sara imagined that, at the end of the day, the teller would remove Sara's $100 dollar bill from the drawer, place it an envelope marked "Sara Wilson," and place the envelope into the bank vault. Sara felt good knowing that her $100 dollar bill would be safe behind that thick vault door.

On the ride home, Sara had doubts. She asked, "Will I get the same $100 bill back when I withdraw my money from the bank?" "No, Sara," her mother explained. "You will get money back, but not the very same $100 bill your grandparents gave you. In fact, you will get more than your $100 back." Sara was shocked!

"Why won't I get my own $100 back?" asked Sara. "Isn't our family bank a safe place to keep money—sort of like a piggy bank for adults? And why would I get more money back than I put in?"

Are banks big piggy banks?

True or False Clues

Read each statement below and mark it true (T) or false (F). Check with your teacher to find out if your responses are correct.

1. Many children get gifts from their grandparents. _____
2. Bank owners keep the money that is deposited in their bank. _____
3. Bank owners make a living by lending money to people who want it to buy a house, buy a car, or open a business. _____
4. In order to make a living, bank owners require that people who borrow money from the bank must pay something extra to the bank. This extra money is called interest. Interest is like a reward to the bank owners for loaning money. _____
5. Bank owners pay depositors some extra money because the bank owners use the deposits to make loans. This extra money is called interest. Interest is like a reward to depositors for putting their money in the bank. _____

The Solution

Solve the mystery, using the clues and ideas from the *Handy Dandy Guide.* Record your solution here and explain it briefly:

_____

_____

_____

Visual 17   How the People of Churchill Came to Be Fond of Polar Bears

Arctic polar bears live for most of the year out on the frozen seas. But in the southern reaches of polar bear country, near Churchill, Manitoba, the bears move inland in July when the ice melts. Then in late fall they head back toward the coast of Hudson Bay. Their migratory route takes them through the town of Churchill, and as they pass through town they cause a certain amount of trouble—eating any dogs they can catch, breaking into houses to check out people's kitchens, and occasionally doing harm to people who cross their path. Until the mid-1980s, people in and around Churchill dealt with the bears by trying to avoid them and by shooting any that got close enough to be a problem.

More recently, however, attitudes have changed. Polar bear hunting is now illegal in Manitoba, and the ban on bear hunting enjoys strong support in Churchill. People there have stopped shooting the bears that still traipse through town every year. In fact, they now go to great lengths to protect polar bears.

What happened? How did the people of Churchill come to be fond of polar bears?

Handy Dandy Guide
1. People *choose* to do the things they think are best for them.
2. People's choices have *costs*.
3. People choose to do things for which they are *rewarded*.
4. People create *rules* that affect our choices and how we act.
5. People gain when they freely decide to *trade* with one another.
6. People's choices today have *future results*.

Activity 17 How the People of Churchill Came to Be Fond of Polar Bears

Directions. Read the *Handy Dandy Guide* and the mystery. For help in solving the mystery, read the clues and decide whether each statement is true or false. Use the clues and ideas from the *Handy Dandy Guide* to figure out a solution to the mystery. Write your solution in the space provided.

Handy Dandy Guide

1. People *choose* to do the things they think are best for them.
2. People's choices have *costs*.
3. People choose to do things for which they are *rewarded*.
4. People create *rules* that affect our choices and how we act.
5. People gain when they freely decide to *trade* with each other.
6. People's choices today have *future results*.

The Mystery

Arctic polar bears live for most of the year on the frozen seas. But in the southern reaches of polar bear country, near Churchill, Manitoba, the bears move inland in July when the ice melts. Then in late fall they head back toward the coast of Hudson Bay. Their migratory route takes them through the town of Churchill, and as they pass through town they cause a certain amount of trouble—eating any dogs they can catch, breaking into houses to check out people's kitchens, and occasionally doing harm to people who cross their path. Until the mid-1980s, people in and around Churchill dealt with the bears by trying to avoid them and by shooting any that got close enough to be a problem.

But more recently, attitudes have changed. Polar bear hunting is now illegal in Manitoba, and the ban on bear hunting enjoys strong support in Churchill. People there have stopped shooting the bears that still traipse through town every year. In fact, they now go to great lengths to protect polar bears.

What happened? How did the people of Churchill come to be fond of polar bears?

True or False Clues

Read each statement below and mark it true (T) or false (F). Check with your teacher to find out if your responses are correct.

1. Polar bears are big, carnivorous animals—on their hind legs, up to 10 feet tall. _____
2. During polar bear migrations, people in Churchill put thick bars over their doors and windows. _____
3. Tourists have little interest in seeing wild animals. _____
4. When tourists visit a particular area, they spend money on motel accommodations, meals, special equipment, and souvenirs. _____
5. Commercial outfitters now offer fall package trips to Churchill, Manitoba, including tundra-buggy outings, dog sled rides, and lectures on environmental topics. _____

The Solution

Solve the mystery, using the clues and ideas from the *Handy Dandy Guide.* Record your solution here and explain it briefly:

_____

_____

_____

_____

Writing Your Own Mysteries

We hope you have had fun thinking about the mysteries we've collected for you. Now we hope to interest you in collecting mysteries of your own.

Our book is open-ended. The world is filled with economic mysteries waiting to be noticed and put to use. You can pick up where we left off. Better yet, you can set your students to the task of finding new mysteries. New ones don't come along every day, but once you and your students get your antennae up you can find enough good mysteries in your time together to enrich your courses considerably. Here are a few suggestions for the task.

Be on the Lookout for Things That Seem Odd

Economic mystery writers pay attention to the news. This is where most of our mysteries come from. While many newspapers and news magazines provide a rich source of possibilities, we have found that the *Wall Street Journal* and the *New York Times* are unusually good sources.

But it isn't enough merely to scan the news in search of stories about economics. The key is to look for oddities, anomalies, curiosities—discrepancies between a reported event or state of affairs and your own sense of what ought to be expected under the circumstances. Discrepancies of this sort invite explanatory efforts; they provide, therefore, excellent focal points for exercises in economic reasoning.

For example, we often read headlines about teacher shortages. Teachers know that shortages do exist. In many states, it is nearly impossible to find a physics or technology teacher. The U.S. Department of Education predicts that we will need 2.2 million new teachers over the next decade.

But teachers also know that there are plenty of new teachers—that there are large surpluses—in some teaching fields. For example, colleges and universities in many states produce surplus numbers of social studies and health teachers. This looks like a mystery. How can we have simultaneous shortages and surpluses of teachers? Can the apparent anomaly be explained by economic reasoning?

Develop a Primary Proposition

Once you have noticed a problem, describe one side of it in a straightforward assertion. We call this a primary proposition. For example:

In 1995, the National Highway Traffic Safety Administration predicted that the expected repeal of the federally mandated 55 miles per hour speed limit would result in an additional 6,400 highway fatalities each year.

The primary proposition states something that is generally known or something that looks reasonable on the face of it. Certainly, it can be difficult to control cars driven at high speeds. It is not surprising, therefore, that allowing states to push speed limits back up to 65 miles per hour seemed like a dangerous idea.

Develop an Opposing Proposition

If you really are onto a good mystery, the facts of the case will suggest information that runs counter to the primary proposition in some interesting way, undercutting it or at least qualifying it. When you come upon counter-examples or counter-arguments of this sort, state them in an opposing proposition, thus implying a mystery or area of uncertainty that needs explaining.

Staying with the speed limit mystery, here is an opposing proposition:

[But] In 1998 the National Highway Traffic Safety Administration announced that fatalities on U.S. highways had fallen to 41,480--down from 41,817 in 1995.

The information conveyed by the opposing proposition runs counter to the prediction (often it is a generalization) reported in the primary proposition. In thinking about opposing propositions, you might find it helpful to notice that it is always possible to begin an opposing proposition with "yet" or "but" or "however."

Identify the Mystery Explicitly

By itself, the juxtaposition of the two main propositions is apt to suggest pretty clearly what the mystery is. But it is important nonetheless to identify that mystery explicitly, so that you know for sure what it is that needs explaining.

Again, staying with the highway safety mystery:

What is going on here? What could explain an observed decrease in automobile crash fatalities following an increase in the legal speed limit?

Focus on Economic Principles in Trying to Explain the Mystery

Set aside non-economic ways of looking at the mystery. Don't trivialize it, for example, by invoking prefabricated cautions about possible measurement problems ("Maybe the new highway statistics are inaccurate") or bias ("Maybe the new Director of the Traffic Safety Administration likes to drive fast"). Measurement problems, observer bias, and other non-economic considerations may fit the facts in a given case, of course, but when they are called upon prematurely or routinely they act as thought-stoppers, preventing people from looking into aspects of the problem that may prove to be far more important and interesting.

The principles of the *Handy Dandy Guide* can help you maintain your economic focus. Those principles highlight, for example, the importance of getting the incentives straight in any analysis of an economic mystery. You may have observed that nearly every one of the economic mysteries in this book can be resolved or clarified in large measure by attention to the incentives at stake. Test the point out against the speed limit mystery. How might a change in highway speed limits alter the incentives that influence the drivers' choices?

Taken together, the *Handy Dandy Guide* principles also highlight the importance of looking beyond what seems obvious. It may seem obvious that if speed limits are increased, more people will be killed on our roads and highways. But in an economic system, one change (a change in incentives, for example) ordinarily leads to several others, with results that can be anything but obvious. In economic reasoning, therefore, we need to keep alert for possible secondary effects or unintended consequences.

Here's the example we've been leading up to—the one about speed limits and highway safety. How might economic principles explain the mystery of fewer deaths at higher speed limits? Let's start at the beginning. Drivers make choices about how fast to drive. Drivers try to make choices that will yield the best combination of costs and benefits. What costs? The cost (in dollars and other losses) of getting hurt in an accident, for example, or the cost of paying for a speeding ticket. Another sort of cost has to do with the value of the driver's time. Getting to destinations faster, or on time according to an anticipated schedule, is an important benefit for many drivers, and it creates an incentive to move along. How fast? It depends on how the driver weighs the potential cost of getting hurt, of getting ticketed, and so on.

Pressing this line of thought further, Stephan Moore of the Cato Institute moved on to the question of why deaths decreased when speed limits went up. According to his analysis, one effect of increasing highway speed limits is to reduce travel times on highways. The prospect of reduced travel time presents drivers with a new incentive. It is an incentive to drive on the highways with higher speed limits, since those highways get you where you're going, faster. But stop and think: *The same incentive encourages drivers to abandon the more dangerous secondary roads.* The shift by drivers to more highway driving might increase *highway* fatalities, but if that increase is offset by a larger decrease in fatalities on the secondary roads, the net effect will be fewer fatalities overall. Notice that this hypothesis is testable. One could look to see whether the fatality rates in question did in fact break down in the manner suggested by Moore's analysis.

Pretty neat, we think. Economic reasoning—guided by an accessible set of principles, and attentive to secondary effects—yields a fresh analysis of a problem and invites further investigation. We hope you and your students will enjoy similar outcomes in your work with economic mysteries.

Let Us Know

We're still collecting mysteries. If you or your students find some good ones, we'd be grateful if you'd let us see them. You can reach us at __mschug@uwm.edu__.